The ABCs to Success

(Simple Words of Wisdom to Live By)

"SimplyStated"
Noreen Baker

Kingdom Builders Publications LLC

© 2020 Noreen Baker

The ABC's to Success

Kingdom Builders Publications, LLC

All rights reserved. No part of this book may be reproduced or transmitted in any form or by any means without written permission from the author.

Printed in the USA

ISBN 978-0-578-64913-9 Soft Cover

LCCN: 2020905378

Authored by
Noreen Baker

Editor
Kingdom Builders Publications

Cover Design
LoMar Designs

DEDICATION

To the Creator who put the vision of words in my heart so I can inspire others.

I dedicate this book to my grandmother; Grandma Donella, my two children; Kristen and Kourtney, my grandson; Kaeden Nyles, my nephews; James Baker, Jr., Marvin Slater, and my first cousin; Terrance Miles.

INTRODUCTION

The ABCs to Success is written to inspire people of all walks of life to live life in its simplest form. It is a wake-up call to say *success* is a process. It won't happen overnight, but if you fashion your time and work ethic into your craft, you will see optimum results. There's no easy way around it; you must put in the time and work to gain advancement and fulfilment. Successful living is about being the best you can be.

This book represents the simple principles I've learned from my grandmother, and I continue to live by them each day. Our success is determined by what we say; what we do; what we think; what we know; and yes, sometimes who we know.

You have what it takes to succeed, however it won't be handed to you. You can make a personal choice to make a personal difference by putting the information in this publication to work. You have the ability to change your life by changing the way you think.

One of the greatest lessons in life is the lesson of LISTENING. Learn to listen to those with knowledge and wisdom, then put it into action by practicing it daily.

My call to action for you is to stay ready for your opportunity. If you're not ready, someone else who was watching and waiting for the chance, will step into your opportunity; all because you were not ready.

I challenge you to learn, do, and reach for your greatest potential. You won't regret it!

Act the part.

Act like whatever you want to become.
Research it. Study it. Find ways to practice it
as often as possible.

B

believe

Believe that you can.

Believe that you have what it takes to make it happen.

Change when needed.

Change is about growing and learning, so you can improve.

D

Don't Quit.

If you feel that it's meant for you, don't quit. Keep working at it.

Evaluate your actions.

Evaluate where you are, where you want to go, and how to get there.

Follow directions.

You will not have all the answers, so seek help and follow the directions.

G

People grow when they try new things.

Grow every day.

Take every day as a new opportunity to learn something new.

Help those in need

Giving back is very important to others and it's good for you.

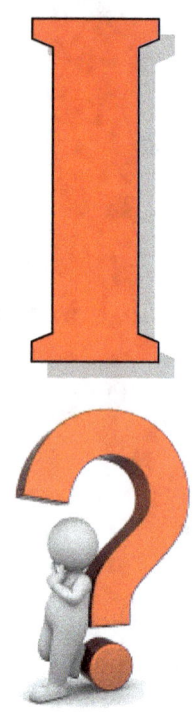

Inquire for knowledge.

Ask when you don't know something. Inquire about it to get the best understanding.

Just do what's right.

Don't be a part of the problem. Even if you have to do it alone.

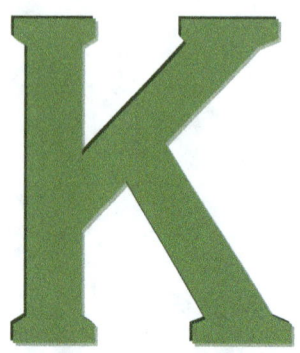

Keep trying.

When it gets tough, keep trying. Don't give up even if you fail……keep trying.

L

LISTEN

Listen more than you talk.

Sometimes you don't need to say anything. You can learn a lot from listening.

M

Mind your manners.

Manners will open doors when nothing else will.

Never give up.

No one can promise that it will be easy. There will be tough times, but never give up.

Open your mind.

Keep an open mind and respect others' thoughts, views and opinions. You may gain some new insight.

Prepare for what you want.

It won't be given to you. You must put in the work.

Q

Quit complaining.

Things will happen and that's life. Go through the process. Learn from it and move forward. Complaining won't change anything. Be a part of the solution!

Rise and shine.

Be ready to begin work when it's time to work.
Sometimes that means getting up early.

Study your craft.

Make your craft a daily practice. Find ways to perfect your skills.

Try

Don't say you can't. Just give it a try.

U

Use your resources.

Think of the people, places and things that you are connected to and can be used as a resource.

Volunteer

Gain experience and knowledge by volunteering. Volunteering has opened doors for many. You will gain skills and knowledge in the process.

W

Work hard.

Giving it your all = strong work ethic.

X

"X" out bad behavior.

You cannot excel with bad behavior.

Y

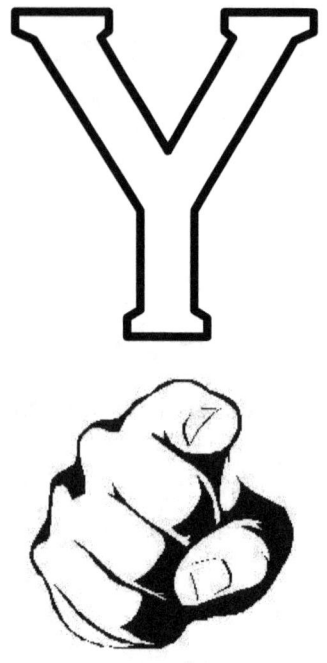

You

There will be things that YOU cannot control,
but YOU can control how YOU react to them.

z

Zap out negative thoughts.

Don't listen to negative thoughts, or let negative thoughts control you. Stay positive by surrounding yourself with positive people.

ABOUT THE AUTHOR

Noreen Baker, born and raised in Darlington, SC.

Her gift of words is inspired by times spent with her grandmother. She enjoyed watching her enjoy life.

She is inspired further by her daughters, grandson, nephews, and cousin who continuously overcome the great demands of life as they journey through adulthood.

She is also inspired to help others move forward by writing words of encouragement based on personal experiences, interactions, places, events, or things.

Noreen's hobbies include reading and writing poetry, calligraphy, tennis, listening to music, exercising, walking, line dancing, watching sports, and helping others.

She has two daughters and one grandchild.

www.ingramcontent.com/pod-product-compliance
Lightning Source LLC
Chambersburg PA
CBHW071415290426
44108CB00014B/1830